THE CONVERSATION EFFECT

STAN SHER

CONTENTS

INTRODUCTION

THE POWER OF COMMUNICATION

"The art of communication is the language of leadership."

> — James Humes

"Leadership is not about being in charge. It is about taking care of those in your charge."

> — Simon Sinek

"The single biggest problem in communication is the illusion that it has taken place."

> — George Bernard Shaw

Communication is the master skill that affects every corner of your life. Whether you're in a boardroom, at the dinner table, negotiating a deal, resolving conflict, or just sharing space with others, how you communicate defines how successful you become.

This book is not about grammar, and it's not just about speaking well. It's about **understanding yourself, reading others, and shifting your mindset** to get what you want by creating alignment. Throughout this journey, you will be challenged to assess your current communication style and develop new ones that enhance both your professional outcomes and personal relationships. The self-realization that occurs when you choose to expand your mindset on this mission will create life-changing outcomes for you. If you have always struggled with conflict with others and it has become a source of frustration for you, now is the time to start examining your behavior. If you're not achieving the results you're looking for in business, it's time to start exploring a better approach.

As you read this book, I want you to be mindful of the fact that I am here to inspire, lead, and coach you into understanding the power of embracing change. This is our journey together, where you are challenged to think with self-awareness as I share stories from my own experiences and the ideologies that elite performers have practiced in this crazy little thing we call life. You see, nothing will ever change, improve, or grow until you decide to take action.

We come from diverse backgrounds, with varied experiences, traumas, and events that have shaped us into who we are. I get very granular sometimes when I think about the actions that create reactions, particularly when it comes to people. I have even analyzed people in my own life, thinking about how they were as children and how they act now as adults. I once had my heart broken by a narcissistic person who forced me to learn some lessons about accepting situations and how to communicate better with people like that. These were lessons that would instill within me so that I would never hurt again.

These days, I am an entrepreneur and have learned to be comfortable in my skin. My self-awareness is very high, and I often reflect on my actions and situations. The personal growth I have experienced in recent years was facilitated by my career as a coach and business consultant. I couple it with some of my studies from the early days, when I took psychology and child psychology classes in college in my pursuit of becoming a schoolteacher. I ended up taking a detour, which eventually led me to make a different stop, resulting in my dropping out of school due to my growing success as an automobile salesperson.

In those days, I was learning to pave the way. I did not use my learning. I adjusted to learning how to engage with people to close sales effectively. Still, it would take many more years until I truly had an appreciation for the art and skill that it creates. I had a manager named Debro Kent at one of my dealerships who was great at analyzing situations and reading people. We would always debrief on the situation whenever we failed to close a sale and discuss aspects such as body language, tone of voice, and even the customer's objections.

As I became a leader at a young age, I took that as one of the first lessons. I became great at this when dealing with business situations, particularly with selling cars. The one thing that would haunt me for the next two decades? My inability to do the same with people in my personal life, and later in business. This inability caused me to ruin relationships when things never went my way and to take things personally. I did not know that if I just learned to calm down, focus on what only I can control, and become naturally curious by asking questions in a properly framed manner, that I would win the day every time! I am sure we have all heard the saying, "You catch more flies with honey than you do with vinegar," when discussing how to win people over. Essentially, this is what we are trying to learn here.

As I write this book, I am fresh from facilitating seminars for over twenty Ford automobile dealerships across North America as part of their "Ford Guest Experience" program. I have personally delivered forty-two full-day immersion programs in four months. Before the tour started, I went through an intense training program where I was treated like a "Guest" by Ford Motor Company while being put through seminars, mindset coaching, simulations with actors where I learned about my shortcomings, reading, self-reflection, and just forced growth. I like to say that I achieved thirty years of personal development in one month.

Some might call it abuse. I call it "growth". I call it "personal development". I call it "the start to my next chapter in life"! The skills I never realized that I possessed started to show. The rejections that I have had in life (business and personal) have escaped me, and they suddenly do not matter anymore. I realized that I was becoming a better communicator and a better reader of situations. Think back to "The Karate Kid" when Daniel thought that "wax on, wax off" and "paint the fence" were a waste of his time until he started to block Mr. Miyagi's attacks flawlessly. That is a discovery!

Communication is what creates everything!

Communication is the difference between being a fantastic friend or family member versus being a terrible person!

Communication separates people from being mediocre to being overachieving success!

If, after reading this book, you track me down and can share one defining moment of self-awareness and/or a life-changing discovery that occurred through improved communication with others, I will feel accomplished and proud that I was a part of your journey of growth. Additionally, there is no shortage of books and media in the marketplace that offer guidance on effective communication. What makes this book unique is that I am talking about this after being alive for four decades and experiencing many setbacks in the past; I grew, and I want to deliver my point of view and inspire you from a different angle.

Thank you from the bottom of my heart for investing in this book. Thank you for taking the time to learn about the lost art of communicating with each other. It is becoming scary in the world as I see people relying on their smartphones and communicating less. What is worse is that it is hard to accomplish nearly anything because either things get ignored or people just take the easiest way. Technology is supposed to make things easier, not harder. The commitment that you make right now to be an effective communicator will ultimately open more doors for you!

Let's get started.

CHAPTER 1

MINDSET IS EVERYTHING

"Whether you think you can, or you think you can't—you're right."

— Henry Ford

Before you say a word, your mindset has already been spoken.

Your thoughts affect how you feel. Your thoughts influence how you communicate. And how you communicate affects what you attract—opportunities, relationships, results, and so on.

If you want to communicate right and win every time, you must first win the conversation happening **in your own head**. I mentioned in the intro earlier about how the lack of specific skills haunted me for decades. This stems from that. When you are growing up and surrounded by situations where financial difficulties are present at home, you often hear constant complaints about how tough things are. Now, before you start thinking otherwise, I grew up in a loving home with hardworking parents who provided the best that they could for me. They never spoiled me, and I earned everything I got.

While my parents were great providers and workers, they never could work on their mindset. When bad news came, they paid attention to the news and their mediocre situations and complained about it. As immigrants coming from Ukraine, they had a very old-school mindset filled with worry and what we can consider negativity. My mother would come up with great ideas, but she never had the mindset to develop a plan and take action. My dad was the leading provider, and he never had the time or energy to develop a mindset that could shield him from negativity; in some cases, he was even deemed a pessimist.

With the old-style thinking filled with worry, they even sheltered me a little, even though they were trying not to. There were worries that my father had that would stop me from taking action when I needed to. For example, I passed on buying a home that would be more than double its current value because of his mindset. Or was it my mindset to take his advice to please him? You see what I did there? Mindset can be not just about you, but someone else's, too. My father was a people pleaser and raised me to be similar. I suppose that when the odds are stacked against you and you're trying to survive, many insecurities will emerge in a person.

That old-school mindset that fosters insecurity also generates considerable doubt and fear in the mind. This fear becomes so profound that it takes over the mind, creating an entirely negative mindset. It puts blinders on, leading a person to often think about the worst-case scenario in everything.

As I grew up and became a professional working with high-performing individuals, such as those earning six and seven figures in the automotive industry, I was introduced to a different way of thinking. I was introduced to the mindset of thinking positively and taking risks in life. I watched people build themselves, attain it all, only to lose it. But then I watched what a strong mindset can do in those situations, as I saw the same people regain everything and then some. As a young and ambitious sales professional trying to find my way, I often spent tens of thousands of dollars investing in myself to attend conferences and seminars, where I could network with the people I wanted to learn from.

There were times when my parents negatively criticized me for dropping out of college or making a career move. I recall 2009, when I quit my six-figure director position in my mid-twenties, and my parents worried about me and what I would do next. My response was always the same: "I will find something soon, and if I don't, I will take a job selling cars and still make a great living because my worst-case scenario is better than most people's best-case scenario, and I'll live with that."

You see, once you gain experience and know how to work a situation, you can follow the same process repeatedly. I went broke three times in my life due to bad business decisions and poor planning (all of which happened due to poor communication skills). Each time I got up and hustled my way back into success. If I had to work two jobs, I would (just as I did in my teens).

How did I condition my mindset to think that way and never feel fear again?

It was all about surrounding myself with successful people who inspired me to believe in myself. One of the first aspects of programming the mindset is to condition yourself to tune out the harmful noise. These days, I clean out my social media feeds once a month because if I don't, I will slowly become part of the problem that society is facing, letting social media ruin us.

Social media is ruining people's minds every moment of the day. It creates heavy insecurity in people and influences them to focus on posting things that will garner attention instead of inspiring them to strive to do and be better in the world.

I am here to tell you that everything can be controlled by the mindset that you give yourself. Until you train your mind to think a certain way and to understand situations, you will not even begin to learn the proper art of communication!

Let's come back to the discussion …

FIXED VS. GROWTH COMMUNICATION MINDSETS

A **fixed mindset** believes "I am who I am" and that skills, habits, and communication styles are static. People with this mindset often say things like:

- "That's just how I talk."
- "I'm not good with people."
- "They just don't get it."

A fixed mindset can even lead to a plethora of excuses, displaying a tightly sealed-off mindset. Just thinking about these three statements, someone who is an effective communicator who possesses natural curiosity can take that conversation further by framing questions such as:

- "What made you talk that way?"
- "Why do you think you are not good with people?"
- "Why is it that they just don't get it?"

A **growth communication mindset**, on the other hand, sees every conversation as a skill to be sharpened, every interaction as a learning opportunity. They say:

- "What can I learn from this?"
- "How could I have handled that differently?"
- "I wonder how they see this."

Notice how much self-awareness and reflection are being brought out by these questions? This is the power of natural curiosity!

Remember how curious you always were as a child about everything? At some point, we all lose that as we develop, but then we subconsciously become too smart for our own good, and we stop asking questions!

REFLECTION PROMPT:

In your last difficult conversation, did you approach it with the intention of proving a point or to learn something new?

This is coming from me, a person who loves to get that last word in. In recent years, I have become more adept at this kind of reflection. For example, I recently dealt with a person who showcases some narcissistic and is a pathological liar (not by choice). I had reached a point where I sometimes no longer wanted to associate with them. It would have felt so justifiable and temporarily satisfying to shout and write a long text message telling them what a narcissist they are. But my reflection prompt to myself was, "Why bother? They would not understand it, nor would they care enough to reflect, because all they know is how to play the victim, and that is why they are what they are."

To elaborate on this reflective prompt...

I made a point to learn something new during one of our last conversations when I asked a series of questions. I read the body language of this person and pieced together pieces from other stories and lies that they had been telling me for eighteen months since we met. From hearing this person's victimized stories, I learned that they were solely the creators of their problems (again, not by choice). I understood why their previous relationships had failed, and I noticed that each of their significant others shared similar negative traits.

What was my ultimate mindset and response?

I saw every possible red flag that I could see. I was immediately hurt for not seeing it sooner, but my life experience had taught me not to dwell on it. My immediate action was to let it go, just as author Mel Robbins discussed in her book. "The Let Them Theory". I could not control the situation. There is nothing I can say or do to improve this situation, except to move on and remove this negativity from my life.

DAILY MINDSET RITUALS

The best communicators don't wait for the world to be in the perfect state before they show up with intention. They **create their state** daily. Take note that everything here is about being aware of yourself and your surroundings. This is what personal accountability looks like.

Here are three mindset rituals you can adopt immediately:

1. Morning Intention Statement

Start each day by saying:

"Today, I choose to listen with curiosity, speak with clarity, and connect with purpose."

2. Pause Before You Respond

Train your brain to insert a moment of silence before reacting. This can be as simple as a breath or a 3-second internal scan:

"Am I reacting or responding?"

3. Evening Reflection

Ask yourself:

- What conversations went well today, and why?
- Where did I let my emotions drive my message?
- What can I improve tomorrow?

Tip: Journal your responses to build awareness over time. (Example: "Something about her expression and tone felt familiar, like past excuses I've heard. Even though I had doubts, I chose to stay curious, asking questions to understand better and possibly recognize a deeper pattern.")

FROM REACTIVE TO PROACTIVE COMMUNICATION

Reactive communication is based on **triggers**. You get defensive. You interrupt. You assume.

Proactive communication is based on **intention**. You ask. You clarify. You listen.

HERE'S HOW TO SHIFT YOUR COMMUNICATION MUSCLE:

Exercise 1: Reframe the Trigger

Think of a recent comment that irritated you. Instead of reacting, ask:

- "What's really bothering me?"
- "What might they be trying to say, even if they said it poorly?"
- "What do I *want* to feel or accomplish in this moment?"
- "If I were observing this interaction, what would I notice?"

Exercise 2: Practice Curiosity Over Judgment

For one day, replace judgmental thoughts with curious questions like:

- "What else could be true?"
- "What are they not saying out loud?"
- "Is there something I'm missing or not seeing clearly?"
- "What would I learn if I asked instead of assuming?"

Exercise 3: Use 'I Wonder' Statements

Instead of jumping to conclusions, try:

- "I wonder why they feel that way."
- "I wonder how I can meet them where they are."

- "I wonder what a calmer version of me would see here."
- "I wonder what they might need that they're not expressing."

FINAL THOUGHT

Communication isn't something you do—it's someone you become. And that begins with your mindset. Even to be self-aware enough to ask these kinds of questions means putting yourself in that mindset. I started joking around, telling the groups of people I facilitate that I sometimes feel like a psychologist because of the types of questions I ask. There are moments when I get people talking, and I can feel the energy of the room. In my work, I strive to maintain a naturally curious mindset, and I am committed to helping others develop their mindset. In my personal life, my mindset is to maintain a caring heart with empathy while understanding that people around me have their motives.

You don't rise to the level of your intentions; you fall to the level of your mental programming.

Upgrade that, and everything else follows.

ACTION PLAN:

Create a "Morning Communication Mantra" you repeat daily. Please write it down right here.

CHAPTER 2

THE LANGUAGE
OF LEADERSHIP

True leaders don't just speak—they **inspire action** through their words.

Think back to the last time a leader's words lit a fire in you—maybe a coach's halftime pep-talk, a manager's "we've got this," or a mentor's quiet faith in your potential. What you remember isn't only *what* they said, it's *how* the message felt. Tone, pace, clarity, and the posture of humble confidence all converged to make the moment stick. In this chapter, we unpack those elements so you can wield them with intention.

One thing I want you to remember is that every one of you is a leader, but you may not always realize it. Take a moment to reflect on the previous chapter about mindset. When I decided not to purchase that home, I was led by my father's influence (or leadership) that came from his mindset (fear and doubt). When I quit my six-figure job without a college degree during a time of uncertainty, I led myself by embracing my mindset of thinking positively and being confident in my abilities. Conversely, leadership can be practiced through structuring conversations with thought-provoking questions while having a visionary mindset.

You may be asking me, "But Stan, what does leadership have to do with communication?"

What you say only matters if you consider how you say it. Have you ever noticed how someone takes control of a conversation, ultimately leading the discussion down a particular path and controlling the narrative? I often talk about being naturally curious. An effective leader in any situation (business or personal) will frequently ask consultative (well-thought-out) questions to elicit the desired response. They will ultimately work to create a clear and confident perception.

It is time to discuss and learn:

- How tone and pace affect perception
- How to lead with clarity, not control
- How to balance confidence with humility

1 THE INVISIBLE SIGNALS: TONE & PACE

1.1 Tone Shapes Emotional Reality

Your tone—or vocal "color"—is the emotional frame around every sentence. The same words, delivered in a warm timbre, invite; delivered flatly, dismiss; delivered sharply, intimidate. Neuroscience shows that listeners evaluate tone *before* they process content, deciding in milliseconds whether to trust, resist, or disengage.

Leader's Lens
- **Empathy Tone:** Slightly softer volume, relaxed pitch changes. Conveys safety.

21

- **Momentum Tone:** Animated inflections, quicker cadence. Signals urgency and possibility.
- **Gravitas Tone:** Lower pitch, measured pauses. Projects steadiness in crisis.

Practice: Record a 60-second message in three tonal styles above. Play it back, noting how your own body reacts—then ask a peer which version compels them to act.

1.2 Pace Controls Perception

- **Deliberate Pace (120–140 wpm):** Lets complex ideas land; shows composure.
- **Up-Shift Pace (160–190 wpm):** Sparks excitement and maintains high energy.
- **Strategic Pauses:** The spoken equivalent of bold font—moments where silence spotlights meaning.

Micro-Drill: Read this next paragraph aloud. Insert a two-second pause before the main takeaway. Notice how the message gains gravity.

"Effective leadership begins with clear, timely communication that turns ideas into coordinated action. When leaders share goals transparently, listen actively, and adapt their message to the audience, they build trust and motivate people to collaborate toward a common purpose."

2 LEAD WITH CLARITY, NOT CONTROL

2.1 Distill, Don't Dilute

Great leaders translate complexity into a single actionable idea. They resist the temptation to flaunt knowledge and instead serve the listener's need for direction.

Clarity Checklist

1. **Headline First:** Open with the core point in one sentence.
2. **Anchor in "Why":** Explain *why* it matters within 20 seconds.
3. **Next Step:** Close with a concrete action or decision.

2.2 Replace Directives with Direction

Control language ("Do exactly this") breeds compliance at best, resentment at worst. Directional language ("Here's the goal; let's explore how") invites ownership. The first part of this will show three examples on a business level, while the second part will incorporate scenarios on a personal level.

Control Phrase (Business Level)	Directional Upgrade (Business Level)
"I need this by noon."	"Let's aim for noon—will that timing set us up for success?"
"Don't make mistakes."	"What checkpoints will ensure accuracy?"
"Follow my plan."	"Here's the framework; add your insights to refine it."

Control Phrase (Personal Level)	Directional Upgrade (Personal Level)
"Take out the trash right now."	"Could you get the trash out before dinner so the kitchen stays fresh?"
"Clean your room this instant."	"Let's have your room tidy before our guests arrive—how can I help you get started?"
"Stop buying coffee every day."	"Can we look at our budget together and decide how that daily coffee fits into our goals?"

Team Huddle Exercise: Present a challenge in directive form. Then restate it directionally. Ask the team which version motivates them and why. First, try it on a business level, and then attempt it at a personal level.

3 BALANCING CONFIDENCE WITH HUMILITY

3.1 The Confidence Signal

Confidence is conveyed before a single syllable: upright posture, steady breathing, and forward resonance. Verbal cues—declarative statements, concrete verbs—cement that signal.

3.2 The Quiet Power of Humility

Humility isn't self-deprecation; it's the willingness to shine the light on others and remain teachable.

Humility in Language

- **Credit-Sharing:** "Our success was possible because of your insights."
- **Curious Inquiry:** "What might I be missing?"
- **Failure Owning:** "Here's where I fell short and what I'm changing."

3.3 The Confidence–Humility Loop

When confidence and humility cycle, trust blooms. Followers see that you believe in the mission *and* value their contribution.

Reflection Prompt (Business Level): Recall a recent win. Craft a two-minute message that both celebrates your role (confidence) and highlights the team's effort or a lesson learned (humility). Deliver it at the next meeting.

Reflection Prompt (Personal Level): Recall a recent success in your life. Think about how it might benefit someone close to you. Craft a two-minute message that both celebrates your role (confidence) and highlights how it can positively benefit that person or group, and let them feel that it is not just about you (humility). Deliver it at the next opportunity.

JOURNAL TIP: – "THREE-LINE LEADERSHIP LOOP"

After every important conversation, write just three quick lines in your journal:

1. **Before** – *What emotion + takeaway did I aim for?*
2. **During** – *Which tone, pace, and humility cue did I choose?*

3.   **After** – *Did listeners reflect the takeaway, and where did engagement dip?*

Keeping it to three focused lines makes the habit sustainable while still capturing the full Pre-Scan → Delivery Map → Debrief cycle. Review a week's entries at once to spot patterns and your next growth edge.

We went through some quick exercises here. My goal was to engage you and add some practicality to this book. Theory is fantastic, but practicing the real deal, there is just nothing like it! I want you to take control of conversations when conducting business and trying to close a transaction. I want you to win every single time you must get something done at home, such as chores, and you need to ask your children to help. You need to become skilled at asking questions and maintaining the proper tone to command respect. Leadership lives in **how** we speak, not just **what** we say. Great communicators read the emotional moment, choose the right vocal style, and frame messages so people want to follow.

Let me elaborate on a little story I mentioned in the introduction about how I was put through a training simulation and how it brought clarity to me. You may recall that earlier, I mentioned I was fresh off a tour with the "Ford Guest Experience," facilitating forty-two immersions. In preparation for this, I attended our T3 (Train the Trainer) event, where we learned how to perform the job and present these immersion training sessions. Our senior leadership hired actors to portray a dealer principal (car dealer owner), a service manager, and a sales manager. Each of them had their own unique style, motivation, goals, personality, and internal challenges within their business.

A group of five of us was put in a room with judges, and we had to conduct a four-minute simulation with each personality to engage with them, make a quick connection, discuss their business, and secure their commitment to send their team for training. Each of them had their objections and had to act out their role as closely as possible in a real-life scenario. Being the friendly rapport builder that I am, I put on my charm to engage in conversation. Most of my conversations went well, but I started to pay attention to body language and responses from others, which forced me to quickly understand what I should have said differently and how I should have framed the conversations.

We were challenged to reflect on what we did well and what we could have done better. These actors gave the most amazing constructive criticism that anyone has ever given me. I took extensive notes and studied them for a whole month. It was life-changing! Just as I am providing you with exercises and practice tips here, I was doing the same for myself. We are halfway through the year, and I wanted to share (with humility and appreciation) this with you. I have fully embraced the "Ford Guest Experience" training, and it has become a part of me. I am proud to say that I consistently achieve high scores with every consulting session I deliver.

This means that if you put your mind to something with a plan to improve, you will achieve your goal. You will become a better leader and a more effective communicator if you practice regularly.

Do not forget that while confidence is essential, we must also be mindful of our audience and how they will perceive us. Effective leaders can read the situation and body language to operate at the same level as their peers. Leaders inspire action by blending clear, listener-centered messages with the right vocal cues and a confident yet humble stance. Master these levers, and every conversation becomes a moment of real influence.

CHAPTER 3

THE COMFORT ZONE DILEMMA

G rowth begins when the familiar ends.

A comfort zone feels like your favorite hoodie: warm, broken-in, reliably "you." Yet wear it in midsummer, and what once soothed now stifles. Communication works the same way. The phrases, audiences, and platforms you default to can quietly limit your influence, even as they keep anxiety low. This chapter reveals why stretching past that invisible border unlocks sharper thinking, deeper connection, and authentic confidence.

BREAKING FREE FROM YOUR COMFORT ZONES

Most of us—myself included—operate inside well-worn comfort zones. They can show up in countless ways, such as:

1. Repeating the same morning routine
2. Dining at the same familiar restaurants
3. Maintaining relationships that no longer serve your growth
4. Remaining in a job you've long wanted to leave
5. Re-creating the same negative situations again and again

These patterns feel safe, yet they quietly restrict potential. The goal of this section is to help you identify those limits and create a path out of them. But to make this fun, let me tell you about one of my comfort zones that even irritates me. I have a terrible habit of not paying attention to what I watch on TV (often forcing me to rewatch something at least three times) because I get addicted to social media, texts, and reels/TikTok that my friends send me. I force myself to get out of my comfort zone by leaving my phone on the charger in another room, so I cannot reach it. I will bet many of you can relate.

Another quick story of being stuck in my comfort zone will shock many people. I despise onions! Since I was born, I have never liked onions in any form. When they are fried, I cannot even stand the smell. It is a habit that my father and I both developed. My friends make fun of me for not liking onions. I love garlic like crazy, though! Anyone who knows me well knows that I love to cook, and for flavor, I use onion powder to reap the benefits of onions. Recently, I decided to step out of my comfort zone! I started creating marinades for meats and poultry to achieve the perfect-tasting grilled meat. I now cut up an onion and add all the ingredients for the marinade, then blend them into a sauce. The results? I now eat onions in some form.

How does it make me feel? I'm eating a healthy ingredient that I've avoided my entire life, and I've found my happy place.

Now I want you to self-reflect and write down the top three comfort zones that you rely on most often. Take five minutes and think deeply about this. Then, I would like you to answer the four prompts. This is also a mindset exercise.

SELF-INVENTORY

List three comfort zones you rely on most often.

1. _____

2. _____

3. _____

Now reflect on each:

Prompt	Your Response
What immediate benefits does this comfort zone provide?	
How does it hold me back— personally and professionally?	
What specific actions can disrupt this pattern in a healthy way?	
How will those actions strengthen me at work and in life?	

Before we go further...

Reflect on what we discussed earlier about framing questions in communication. Do you notice how they were asked? It is simple! Dr. Stephen Covey said, "seek first to understand, then to be understood" as his 5th habit in the best-selling book, "The 7 Habits of Highly Effective People." The questions that you just answered are an example of the level of communication skills that you seek.

GATHER SUPPORT

Stepping beyond the familiar can feel daunting. That's why even world-class performers rely on coaches, mentors, or peers to guide and encourage them. Let's face it! This is why you invested in this book. **Do understand that this is your journey, and growth takes commitment and practice to achieve.**

Do not attempt a significant change entirely on your own (in some cases). Identify at least one person or group who can offer feedback, accountability, or simply a different perspective. For communication excellence, I can confidently say that joining a local Toastmasters International group (https://www.toast-masters.org) will be one of the best decisions you ever make. Toastmasters has changed my life and helped me get started when I was not capable or confident as a speaker. It helped me create a network of friends and business professionals as well.

Speaking of getting out of comfort zones within this topic. I once owned a social media marketing firm called "Social Sher," where we helped several brands become nationally recognized, including a few automobile dealerships, a guitar accessories company, a restaurant, and a barber shop. The dilemma we faced was that none of our clients wanted to be on video, or were too shy. Many times, we would spend hours filming hundreds of takes. My business partner, who was also the cameraman, finally got fed up and said, "You do it for them and be the star". I got in front of the camera and became "Social Sher," where I would deliver a message in just one take and move on. All you had to do was educate me on something in a few short minutes, and just like AI, I would craft a message in real time on video and move on.

In sales, a closer steps in when the original rep has gone as far as they can. The second voice, style, or strategy often seals the deal. The same principle applies to personal growth: a fresh viewpoint can unlock what you couldn't reach on your own.

Ask yourself:

- Who in my network can challenge my thinking and support my next move?
- What conversations or introductions could open new possibilities?

Growth begins the moment you pair internal resolve with external support. Use both to move decisively beyond your comfort zones and into sustained progress.

As I put a bow on this chapter, I want you to think back to the three comfort zones that you chose. I want to tell you that staying where you excel can inflate "situational confidence." The danger lies in removing the familiar variables—different culture, medium, or stakes—and that confidence evaporates. True confidence is transferable; it only develops through varied reps. Stepping out of your comfort zone will sharpen clarity and connection for you.

JOURNAL TIP – "STRETCH STAMP"

At the end of each day, add a quick **"Stretch Stamp"** to your journal:

1. **Zone Spotted:** *Where did I feel most comfortable today?*
2. **Stretch Attempted:** *What single action nudged me outside that zone?*
3. **Result & Insight (1-2 lines):** *What did I learn or gain from the discomfort?*

CHAPTER 4

ASSUMPTIONS:
THE SILENT SABOTEUR

We destroy the connection by assuming.

I bet every one of you has been in a situation like this…
Camille watched her teammate Jordan shrug during a project review and instantly concluded he disliked her idea. Irritated, she cut their collaboration short and revised the plan alone. Two days later, she discovered Jordan's shrug had nothing to do with her proposal—he'd just received news of a family emergency. Camille's quick assumption cost them time, strained the relationship, and almost derailed the project. Situations like this play out daily in homes, offices, and friendships, eroding trust in small, silent increments.

Now, let's dive into my personal experience with the narcissistic tendencies. The first time I wanted to cut them out of my life, I already knew some truths, and I delivered that very long text message, not realizing I was dealing with someone who is not being self-aware of their actions. I was hoping this person would have a response, but I learned that it doesn't faze them. However, what I did was outline several assumptions based on this person's history of lying and manipulating others. We hadn't spoken for almost three months.

One day, we reconnected, and then they told me how they felt like I had made a lot of unproven assumptions. Here I am teaching this stuff to people, and I found myself making assumptions. In my defense, I did read the situation right, and at least half of my assumptions were correct, as I would later find out. Yet I still made mistakes by making assumptions.

In business, we often make assumptions when judging a book by its cover. When I was selling automobiles and was new to the industry, I had guests (customers) thrown at me by veteran sales consultants who judged everyone who walked in. I worked harder on those deals, but I sold them while my colleagues looked foolish. I had a customer purchase a vehicle from me because I treated him with respect and as a guest, while our biggest competitor spoke down to him. This customer was wealthy and made more money than our entire sales department combined. He was dressed down, working from home, and was humble enough not to flaunt his wealth.

SPOTLIGHT EXERCISE – ASSUMPTION IN ACTION

We are all born with a reflex to fill in the blanks. When we see someone who looks unhappy, frustrated, or simply "off," our brains race to explain why, that lightning-fast story feels useful—yet it is almost always incomplete.

Look at the photo.

What story springs to mind about this person's mood or situation?

Now let's debrief.

What narrative are you crafting for them?

Thought experiment: Suppose this individual is hard of hearing. On top of that, each is dealing with a private setback—yet right now, they have to rely on you to get something done. How might those unseen factors change the way you engage them?

SCENARIO 1 (BUSINESS): THE $1,000 CELL-PHONE BUYER

You're working at ABC Wireless. A customer walks in to spend more than a thousand dollars on a new phone. Their shoulders sag; their expression says anything but excitement.

Your instinct might be:

"They're angry at the price."
"They must hate shopping."
"Something someone did annoyed them."
"They must be miserable, how lucky am I today?"

But none of those stories are confirmed facts. Instead, try opening with curiosity and immediate empathy:

1. "Welcome to ABC Wireless; my name is Stan. How can I make your day better?"
2. "Hi, I'm Stan. How can I best serve you today?"
3. "Hello, I'm Stan. Welcome to our home. How can I deliver the best guest experience for you today?"

These lines do three critical things:

- **Acknowledge** the person as more than a transaction.
- **Invite** them to share real context before you guess.
- **Signal expertise** by focusing on service, not assumptions.

SCENARIO 2 (PERSONAL): THE QUIET FRIEND ON YOUR COUCH

Your best friend drops by unannounced and sinks into your sofa. They stare at the floor, scrolling their phone, barely looking up when you walk in.

Your instinct might be:

- "They're mad at me for something."
- "Maybe they're bored and want attention."

- "Something awful must have happened at work."
- "Great, now I have to play therapist."

But none of those stories are confirmed facts. Instead, try opening with curiosity and immediate empathy:

1. "Hey, I'm really glad you're here. How can I make this moment better for you?"
2. "I've got time and ears—what would feel most helpful right now?"
3. "I care about you. What do you need from me in this moment—space, a snack, or just someone to listen?"

These lines do three critical things:

- **Acknowledge** your friend as a whole person, not a problem to fix.
- **Invite** them to share the real context before you assume.
- **Signal support** by centering their needs, not your own interpretation.

WHY THIS MATTERS

In business, when a guest (customer/client) feels safe to talk and senses you are listening, a sale becomes a relationship. And relationships, not one-off wins, build lifelong business and personal goodwill. On an individual level, when you get curious and upfront about being there for your friend by asking thoughtful questions, you will connect with them and win.

Breaking the assumption habit is hardwired work; our brains crave quick conclusions. The antidote is **self-awareness** coupled with deliberate, curiosity-based language. Each time you notice an untested story—pause, ask, and listen.

REFLECTION PROMPT

How could a single welcoming question from you flip someone's difficult day into one of relief and gratitude? Jot one recent encounter where curiosity could have replaced assumption, and script the opening line you'll use next time.

My challenge to you, as this part of the journey comes to an end, is to pay close attention to when you are about to make an unproven assumption. Get self-aware in the moment and just stop yourself, think quickly, and ask a consultative question or two. Take note of the response and learn from the positive effects of this interaction. Making assumptions is generally negative because it can create anger, hostility, and uncomfortable situations for everyone (depending on personalities).

On the other hand, reading people and situations can also create assumptions. Can the art of making assumptions have a positive effect when we are reading a situation? It worked with over a 50% success rate when I dealt with that narcissist!

Do you understand why timing, self-awareness, and acting matter now? To become competent in communication, you should now have a basic understanding of the steps to achieve this goal.

CHAPTER 5

BECOME THE LEADER
OF THE MOMENT

L eadership isn't a title—it's a decision.

A decision comes from having the properly programmed mindset. A title can open doors, but only a decision opens minds. In every conversation—whether you're closing a deal, wrangling toddlers, or calming a panicked coworker—there is a split-second window where the room looks for direction. That window belongs to whoever **decides** to take it. This chapter gives you a goal to program your mindset to seize that window, **own the moment**, and guide everyone through the fog of confusion or chaos.

Leadership also involves being self-accountable for how we process thoughts in our minds. There are so many aspects to leadership. One of my favorite aspects of being a leader is the ability to be resilient, survive uncertain situations, and thrive at peak levels. So why do I bring up resilience in a book about communication? Effective communication is developed over time. Our experiences shape what we become. They make us stronger and allow us to share the wisdom we have gained.

How can I write this book and talk about these ideologies?

I have had to be resilient many times in my life, particularly when I failed at something or did not communicate effectively. At one point in my life, my automotive training and consulting business was on the verge of collapse. I wanted to blame everyone, from my competitors to clients, not seeing the value. I was young, full of energy, and anger. I picked social media battles with the wrong people. It hurt my brand big time. I even got sued by a competitor in business who was also a mentor to me. This lawsuit could have been resolved over a simple steak dinner instead of a court battle.

What was the real problem? Me! I had an ego and wanted to prove myself to the world how macho I was. It wasn't a great practice. I spent a few years being sour and angry. As I shifted my mindset to be self-aware and focus on what matters in life, I took stock of what I can control, and I mended fences with many with whom I had battled. I learned how to communicate more effectively and not be self-serving, but instead focus on serving others.

COMMUNICATION IS LEADERSHIP IN ACTION

Leadership doesn't begin with a promotion, a title, or a nameplate on your desk. It starts with **a decision**—a decision to take control of the energy in the room, the clarity in the conversation, and the next best step forward.

In any moment of uncertainty—when emotions are high, silence is awkward, or direction is unclear—the most influential communicator is the one who steps up to bring order, clarity, and calm. That person becomes the leader, even if no one ever formally declared it.

This chapter is about becoming that person. We are going to explore two scenarios here that will similarly happen in our lives at some point. These are real-world examples.

SCENARIO 1 (PERSONAL): THE WEEKEND CAMPING TRIP

Let's imagine five friends decide to go on a weekend camping trip. The idea sounds exciting to everyone, but most in the group are simply saying, "Just let me know what I need to bring."

There's no clear plan for:

- Where to go
- What gear to bring
- Who's driving
- What meals will be
- How will the costs be split

Someone needs to step up—not with control, but with **clarity**. This person becomes the *unofficial trip leader*, taking the initiative to map out the logistics, create a shared checklist, and ensure everyone's preferences are considered. They ask questions like:

- "Does everyone prefer rustic or comfort camping?"
- "Any food allergies or must-have snacks?"
- "How about we split the cost of supplies evenly?"

To keep things on track, they set up a group text thread or shared document where tasks like grocery shopping, tent packing, and gathering firewood are delegated.

This friend may not have asked for the leadership role, but they **decided** to seize the moment, allowing everyone to have a great time.

The result?

Less confusion. More fun. No one shows up without a sleeping bag. And most importantly, **everyone feels seen and included—** all because one person communicated with purpose.

SCENARIO 2 (BUSINESS): LAUNCHING A NEW PRODUCT CAMPAIGN

Let's imagine a cross-functional team of five coworkers is tasked with launching a new product. While everyone has a role—marketing, design, sales, finance, and operations—most contribute their part and wait for direction.

Someone must step up to **own the moment** and lead the execution. This person becomes the informal project lead, coordinating timelines, clarifying goals, managing expectations, and ensuring the entire team delivers a unified and compelling launch.

To be successful, this leader must understand the unique strengths and communication styles of each team member. Effective communication becomes essential, not just during meetings but **between them**. Setting up a shared workspace (such as Slack, Teams, or Asana) and initiating weekly checkpoints helps everyone stay informed and accountable.

Just like a well-planned camping trip, a successful campaign requires:

- **Mapped milestones** (timelines & deliverables)
- **Shared vision** (what success looks like)
- **Budget clarity** (spend tracking)
- **Constant communication** (everyone on the same page)

Leadership here is not a title—it's the courage to coordinate, communicate, and care about the outcome.

THE COMMUNICATION-LEADER MINDSET

In every communication exchange, especially the difficult ones, people are silently asking:

- Who here knows what to do?
- Who can help me make sense of this?
- Who's going to lead us forward?

When no one steps up, people panic, freeze, or fumble. But when one person assumes responsibility—not for knowing everything, but for guiding the next step—people lean in and follow. It is easy for people to become followers and rely on someone else's leadership. Leadership is not for everyone. This is why some people are employers and others are employees. This is also why some people achieve their goals, while others struggle. Again, it all stems from mindset.

Once I discovered the benefits of commanding a conversation and asking questions, I was able to achieve what I was looking for. This made me a great closer when selling cars and even a better appointment setter in business development centers in auto dealerships. This is the mindset and skills that I bring to organizations when they hire me to deliver coaching to their teams.

Before we proceed and start making assumptions about the dangers of this, I want to emphasize that it is always essential to be ethical when engaging in these conversations. Do not go out and learn deadly sales closes that will be used to manipulate people. There is a vast difference between effective communication and manipulation. The power of persuasion should be used positively to help others see things from a different perspective.

Leadership begins when you decide to guide the moment, not control the people.

MOMENTS THAT NEED A COMMUNICATOR-LEADER

You don't need to be the manager, CEO, or team captain to step into leadership. The opportunity to lead can happen:

- When a team meeting drifts into confusion
- When a customer raises their voice or breaks down
- When friends are arguing and nobody's listening
- When a project stalls because no one's taking ownership
- When a loved one is overwhelmed and needs direction

In each of these moments, the quality of your **communication** determines whether you create calm or contribute to chaos. The key is to have the right mindset and strike a balance between comfort and confidence. When all else fails, ask some questions!

OWN THE MOMENT: A 3-STEP LEADERSHIP COMMUNICATION MODEL

1. Pause & Presence

The first step to leadership is not speaking—it's pausing.

Center yourself. Slow your breath. Make eye contact. Before words even leave your mouth, your presence communicates, *"I'm grounded. I've got this."*

This sets the tone for others. People don't follow the loudest voice—they follow the calmest energy.

2. Clarify & Align

The second step is identifying the root of the issue. Use clear, inclusive language:

- "What I'm hearing is that we're unclear on the next step."
- "Sounds like we're all frustrated, but for different reasons. Let's unpack that."
- "Let me repeat what I believe we're trying to accomplish."

Clarity builds trust. Alignment invites collaboration.

3. Guide & Move Forward

Once clarity is established, take the next best communicative step:

- Ask a decisive question: "Can we all agree this is our priority for today?"
- Assign roles: "Would you be willing to capture our ideas as we brainstorm?"
- Set a path: "Let's commit to the next 10 minutes sorting solutions, not assigning blame."

This isn't about being a dictator. It's about guiding the process, not dominating it. This is what having control is all about. The goal is to resolve a conflict maturely before it starts. Ever see someone be so slick with their words that they have been able to talk themselves out of a traffic violation or out of overpaying for something? They did it because they took control of the situation and said all the right things.

Here is a real-life example of how things can deteriorate rapidly. The other day, when I was at my community pool, a conflict arose. The supervisor for the pool management company walked in to check on the lifeguard. She randomly told a resident that their inflatable floating device was not allowed in the pool.

Oddly enough, there was never a rule such as this imposed or written out. It was news to the resident. This resident began to get defensive and started saying phrases that triggered the supervisor to respond with statements like, "I understand that you do not agree with this, and you are entitled to your opinion." All that did was escalate the resident's anger to the point where she started shouting at her. The conversation unpacked other issues where the supervisor asked her for her name, only to be told, "You don't need my name, I live around the corner."

This escalated into a major conflict, as the supervisor's careless words only made the resident angrier. This conflict turned into drama.

In this case, neither party was trained in effective communication. This could have escalated, potentially into a physical altercation, as the resident shouted, "Get out of my face." The supervisor was a terrible leader. She threw her lifeguard under the bus, explaining that these lifeguards are so young and do not have the backbone to assert their authority to speak up.

I sat back and watched this pointless exchange of drama, analyzing the situation. I even told one of my neighbors that "the problem here is that both of them do not know how to communicate with others properly, and this battle could be avoided." I enjoyed this experience, as it helped prepare me to write this book. So here is how I would have reacted in this situation from both parties' perspectives.

Supervisor Role: I would approach the resident and initiate a conversation in a friendly manner. I would say things like, "Hello, how is your day going? Are you enjoying the weather?" followed by quietly saying things like, "I am not sure if we made all the residents aware or not, but for this summer, the association does not allow flotation devices. Can you please remove it from the pool for now?"

Resident Role: Here is how I would respond to the situation as I read it. "Hi, all is great. Thank you. I'm just happy we finally had some sunny days. Hope all is well with you. Wow. I had no idea they had introduced this new rule. I wish they had done a better job communicating with us. I understand where you are coming from. I will remove it for now. However, I am curious, and I know this is not your responsibility. This rule does not make much sense, and it is harmless, so I would like to address it. Who should I talk to about this rule?"

Do you see what happens when two mature adults can speak kindly to one another? There is way too much uncertainty in this world, and much of it comes from communication conflict.

Now, please consider some of the benefits of approaching this situation mindfully and diplomatically. Approaching the situation in this way can prevent the resident from getting triggered, and the problem can be resolved quickly. Notice how the conversation becomes smoother when the supervisor approaches the resident in a friendly, empathetic, and personable manner. The resident is less likely to snap, lose her temper, and get defensive.

If the resident were calmer and took a few seconds to analyze the situation, they would be able to acknowledge the statement kindly without an argument breaking out. A significant benefit of this would be that less frustration would occur, and other internal issues would not need to be addressed in public. Sometimes, just smiling and addressing a statement with kindness can go a long way.

LEADERSHIP SCRIPTS FOR THE MOMENT

Here are some plug-and-play phrases to use when the moment needs direction:

- **"Let me help us reset this."**
- **"What would make this clearer for everyone?"**

- "Here's what I believe is the most important thing right now."
- "Let's agree on one small next step."
- "Before we react, can we reflect for a second?"
- "Hey, I care about where this is going—can we take a breath and just talk this through?"
- "This matters to me. Let's try again, but with less heat and more heart."
- "I know we both want a good outcome here. What's one thing we can agree on before we keep going?"

These lines shift the energy. They move the conversation from reaction to intention, from conflict to clarity.

Communication Excellence = Leadership in Every Moment

Owning the moment isn't about being the smartest, most experienced, or most senior person in the room. It's about choosing to communicate with clarity, empathy, and purpose—especially when others won't.

So the next time you're in a room full of confusion, silence, or stress, don't ask, *"Why isn't someone fixing this?"*

Instead, ask, *"How can I lead this moment with communication that brings clarity and calm?"*

And then **decide to do it. After all, being effective means striving for better, and that comes from being self-aware and the decision to act on being the leader of the situation.**

CHAPTER 6

SELF-AWARENESS AND EMOTIONAL MASTERY

"Until you make the unconscious conscious, it
will direct your life—and you will call it fate."

— *Carl Jung*

You can't master communication if you don't master your emotions.

Whether in a heated argument, a high-stakes negotiation, or a personal heart-to-heart, communication is never just about the words. It's about energy, tone, timing, body language, and—most importantly—emotions.

If you want to become a master communicator, you must first become a master of yourself.

This chapter gives you the tools to identify, regulate, and channel your emotions—so your words come from intention, not impulse. Let's dive into the work of emotional mastery.

Consider the story I told in the previous chapter, where my neighbor got into a heated argument with the pool supervisor. Think about how emotional it got for both parties and how the impulse caused the resident to flip out. I am the first to admit that I sometimes tend to react like that, too. We all naturally can act like this if we do not control ourselves.

1. EMOTIONAL INTELLIGENCE: THE ENGINE BEHIND EFFECTIVE MESSAGING

Emotional Intelligence (EQ) is your ability to understand and manage your emotions and recognize and respond to the feelings of others. It's what allows you to:

- Stay calm under pressure
- Deliver hard truths with compassion
- Read the room and shift your delivery accordingly
- Create psychological safety in conversations
- Influence outcomes without manipulation

High EQ communicators are not only heard—they're trusted. This is how we can condition ourselves to be more calculated. When I took notes during the simulation of role-playing scenarios with those actors, I put a significant emphasis on studying emotional intelligence. I paid attention to how someone reacted when I asked a question in a specific manner. When I asked the narcissistic person certain questions, I paid attention to what was being avoided and how they were telling a lie (when I was well informed of the truth right before it), which they wanted to use to manipulate me.

THE FOUR PILLARS OF EQ IN COMMUNICATION

1. **Self-Awareness** – Recognize your emotional state before you speak.

2. **Self-Regulation** – Manage impulses and choose your tone intentionally.

3. **Social Awareness** – Read the emotional cues of others in the moment.

4. **Relationship Management** – Utilize empathy, timing, and tact to guide interactions effectively.

💡 **Pro Tip:** Before any important conversation, ask yourself:

- What emotion am I carrying into this?
- Will that emotion serve or sabotage the outcome?

Since starting to work on myself, I have developed a practice to set my mindset to be in the moment. I recognize how I'm feeling, and I condition myself to take whatever comes back at me with a grain of salt. To take it a step further, I remind myself of the impulses the other party is known to have historically. It is possible to become deadly when using well-thought-out relationship management techniques at that moment.

The best way to learn from this is to debrief on previous interactions with people who were defensive, combative, impulsive, and even egotistical. As an exercise, jot down some notes reflecting on body language, tone, level of response, and more.

3. COMMUNICATING EMOTIONS AUTHENTICALLY

Authentic communication doesn't mean emotional dumping. It means expressing emotions **with responsibility**, not blame.

Say This, Not That:

Instead of...	Try saying...
"You're making me mad."	"I'm feeling frustrated and need clarity."
"You don't care about me."	"I feel disconnected and want to understand where we're at."
"I can't deal with this right now!"	"I need a moment to collect my thoughts before we continue."

When you own your emotions, you protect the relationship, even in conflict. When you make it about yourself instead of them and own it, you can frame statements effectively. Stop blaming others and making statements that will offend them and lead to confrontation. Once again, this will require an open mind and self-awareness.

I was once engaged and in a very long relationship. Throughout the time we were together, I emphasized becoming a better business consultant by improving my communication skills. The high-level consulting projects I worked on with major automobile manufacturers, such as Hyundai and Ford, required extensive training. I found myself coming home and handling conflict with my ex-fiancé in a manner that was consultative and respectful. Whenever she found a reason to blame someone else or me, I threw back questions to get her talking. The problem? She was astute and a great judge of character, so she would call me out and say things like, "Stop trying to facilitate me and acting like a robot."

I had significant others tell me things like "stop acting like a car salesman and manipulating the situation." These skills can be a blessing or a curse, but at least I was reminded that I am naturally putting them into practice. Once again, I remind everyone not to use this for manipulation, but to manage the situation effectively.

4. THE COST OF EMOTIONAL IMMATURITY

When you ignore, suppress, or mismanage your emotions, your communication becomes:

- Defensive
- Confusing
- Dismissive
- Reactive
- Manipulative

And once you damage trust through uncontrolled emotions, words often lose their power.

People remember how you made them feel—especially when your tone didn't match your message. The supervisor at my pool had a negative approach to how she interacted with the resident in the story that I told. The resident got defensive and reactive. The biggest issue in managing emotional immaturity in humans is that we often fail to take the time to study our communication patterns. Our parents do not teach us this, and we grow up with habits that were never concentrated on.

REAL-WORLD SCENARIO (BUSINESS): THE DISAPPOINTED MANAGER

A team misses a major deadline. The manager is furious, but pauses before storming into the room.

She steps into her office, takes three deep breaths, and silently names her emotion: *"I'm angry because this affects the company's reputation."*

Instead of exploding, she says:

"I'm upset about the missed deadline. Before we unpack what went wrong, I want to hear from each of you about what got in the way. My goal isn't to assign blame, but to understand and improve."

This is emotional mastery. It transforms tension into trust— and builds stronger teams.

REAL-WORLD SCENARIO (PERSONAL): THE OVERWHELMED PARTNER

You walk into the kitchen after a long, stressful day to find dishes piled up, laundry still unfolded, and your partner watching TV. Instantly, you feel a surge of frustration rising. Your inner dialogue starts firing:

"I've been working all day, and they're just relaxing?"
"I'm doing everything around here!"

You're about to snap—but instead, you catch yourself.

You step into the hallway, take three deep breaths, and silently name your emotion:

"I'm frustrated because I feel unsupported and exhausted."

When you return to the room, you say calmly:

"I'm feeling overwhelmed right now. I had a long day and was hoping to come home to a bit more support. Can we talk about how we can divide things up better so we both feel good at the end of the day?"

This is emotional mastery in action.

It's not about suppressing how you feel—it's about **owning it**, naming it, and choosing how you express it.

And in doing so, you turn potential conflict into a deeper connection.

6. REFLECTION QUESTIONS

- What emotional habits do I default to (shutting down, snapping, avoiding)?
- How do those patterns affect my relationships and reputation?
- When was the last time I paused before reacting—and how did that change the outcome?
- What "emotional triggers" do I need to become more aware of?

I urge you to put these questions into practice. The younger, immature version of myself was not mindful of this, and it set me back many years. This is how I burned through some relationships and damaged my business in the early days. The good news for all of us is that there are second chances in life to learn, improve, grow, and adjust to doing things right. The time for you is right here and right now!

ACTION PLAN: TRAIN YOUR EMOTIONAL INTELLIGENCE

Week	Focus	Daily Practice
1	Self-Awareness	Journal 3x/day: What am I feeling and why?
2	Self-Regulation	Use a 10-second pause before every hard reply.
3	Empathetic Listening	Mirror back what someone else said before responding.
4	Authentic Expression	Share one real emotion daily—with tact and ownership.

CHAPTER 7

THE ART OF LISTENING AND OBSERVING

"The most important thing in communication is hearing what isn't said."

— *Peter Drucker*

Most people listen to reply. Leaders listen to **understand**.

In a world filled with noise, authentic listening has become rare and powerful. When someone feels deeply heard, they don't just open up—they lean in, trust more, and often find their answers in the space you hold.

This chapter is about becoming the kind of communicator whose presence speaks louder than their voice. You'll learn how to listen with your ears, your eyes, and your intuition. The result? A level of influence and trust that can't be manufactured through clever words alone.

I used to act without listening. When I started working as a sales consultant at the car dealership, I used to fight whatever I was told to do with customers. I used to question everything and disagree in a combative way. Here I am, a green pea with no experience in anything, being told by my manager to approach a customer, and I'm doing the opposite - not getting the result

I'm looking for. My managers, who had decades of experience, were trying to coach me, but I was ignoring their guidance. The lesson here is that when someone more successful than you is offering advice, it makes more sense to listen and adapt to them. My friend and colleague, Nato Di Bella, used to remind me that I was born with two ears and one mouth.

As I learned to adapt to those strategies, I would notice my father saying things to me like, "Don't start acting stupid like those guys." I would say things in return, like, "What makes this stupid? These are habits of successful people doing better than me in life." My mindset shifted, and I too became like my fellow car enthusiasts in the business. What happens is that we become who and what we surround ourselves with. What might look ridiculous to the average person is just a way of life for people who work in the retail automobile industry.

When I began to transition from retail to training and consulting, I surrounded myself with industry colleagues and partners who were known for changing the game. I can think of at least five people that I can call right now who have built massive organizations and had successful nine-figure exits. These are the people that I started to listen to and take advice from. I observed what these people do and picked up on some of their habits both in business and in their personal lives.

We all need someone to look up to and learn from. However, the mindset needs to be that we must learn from someone who has successfully done it. If you are going to ask for advice about the secret to keeping a marriage going for fifty years, it's probably wise to talk to someone who has done it. If we want to learn how to lose weight, gain muscle, and become a strong, healthy version of ourselves, we are not going to take advice from someone who is overweight.

1. THREE LEVELS OF LISTENING

Let's break down the layers of listening and how each impacts connection.

A. Surface Listening

- You hear the words but don't absorb the meaning.
- Your mind is formulating your next reply or is distracted.
- Most people live here—and it's why so many conversations go in circles.

"Yeah, I heard you." ≠ "I understand you."

Most conversations today suffer from what we call **surface listening**—the kind of listening that technically hears the words but misses the message. It's a habitual, reactive state of partial presence. Let me be blunt and say that this tends to happen when the other person is displaying ignorance. This also happens to people who display narcissism.

B. Active Listening

- You give verbal cues ("Mhm," "I see," "Go on").
- You paraphrase to confirm understanding.
- You ask clarifying questions to invite more depth.

This builds trust, but it's still focused on information exchange—not transformation.

C. Deep Listening

- You're not just listening to words—you're listening for meaning, emotion, and energy.
- You hold silence without rushing to speak.
- You reflect back not just *what* they said but *how* they said it.

This is where emotional breakthroughs, healing conversations, and transformational leadership happen.

💡 **Try this:** The next time someone talks to you, respond not with advice, but with:

"That sounds important—tell me more."

But what about silence?

Do you ever just sit quietly and observe your surroundings? What scenario are you laser-focused on? What observations are you making?

You see, silence can be one of the most intelligent and deadly practices that a person can do. Silence can very well be used to think, or it can be used to act in a nonchalant way. We do not always need to speak or think out loud. Sometimes the simple act of being quiet will get you where you need to go.

The way that a person simply does not respond to a text message is an example of a response. They might be telling you that they do not care, have something to hide, answer the question by avoiding it, and many other ways, all by just not responding. On the other hand, a triggered person who cannot help but express emotions can go on a long rant because they are not able to manage themselves. The only real thing to understand here is that we need to be better at reading situations and understanding the concept.

When the concept of listening and understanding becomes part of our normal practice, we will start to understand ourselves as well as other people. One might argue that practicing these concepts might avoid confrontation and bring better peace within ourselves.

SILENCE AS COMMUNICATION

Business Example:

In a team meeting, the manager asks, *"Does anyone see any issues with this project timeline?"* Everyone stays silent. That silence may not mean agreement—it could be signaling fear of speaking up, lack of confidence, or unspoken disagreement. The smart manager interprets the silence and follows up with, *"I'd like to hear concerns privately after this meeting if anyone isn't comfortable speaking now."*

Personal Example:

During an argument at home, one partner stops talking, crosses their arms, and avoids eye contact. The silence communicates frustration, withdrawal, or needing space—without a single word.

TRIGGERED WORDS AS COMMUNICATION

Business Example:

An employee feels overlooked for a promotion and starts venting to HR:

"I've been here longer than half the people who got promoted! I'm always the one staying late and cleaning up messes! Nobody notices how much I do!"

Although it comes out emotionally, the outburst communicates feelings of being undervalued and unseen—valuable feedback if handled with empathy.

Personal Example:

At a family dinner, a sibling feels criticized and goes on and on:

"You're always judging me! I can't do anything right! No matter what I accomplish, you compare me to everyone else!"

The flood of words reveals deeper pain—desire for acceptance and recognition.

☞ In both silence and emotional venting, the message isn't in the words alone—it's in the meaning beneath them.

We are all built with complexities. It goes back to how we are taught, raised, conditioned, and the habits that we form. The habits we are raised with often become the foundation of how we think, act, and respond in life. Whether good or bad, they shape our discipline, our mindset, and even the way we see the world. As adults, it's up to us to recognize which habits to carry forward, which to break, and which new ones to build in order to grow into the person we want to become. This is why sometimes in communications the wisest action is to be silent.

CHAPTER 8

FRAME IT RIGHT:
QUESTIONS OVER ANSWERS

"The smartest person in the room isn't the one
with the best answers—it's the one who asks the
questions that change the conversation."
- Stan Sher

Being right isn't always effective. The most powerful communicators know that questions do more than gather information—they build trust, uncover hidden needs, and guide conversations toward meaningful outcomes. Answers can close doors, but questions open them.

How did I learn this lesson?

I had been consulting for a business for over a decade and thought that I was decent at my craft. I had started working on a consulting project for Hyundai Motors of America. During my onboarding, I was visiting dealerships with a seasoned consultant whose dealerships I was going to start working with. Jeff was the consultant. I noticed that Jeff was asking some commonsense questions about the framing of this dealer's website, but I had no idea why he asked those questions.

I jumped in with my expertise and started to answer the question while sharing best practices. I was not trying to be smart or show it, but I felt like I was helping them. Jeff had brought me to the side and explained the concept in five minutes to me as to why he asked the question and what he was trying to achieve. This immediately changed my mindset and how I would forever operate. I would become consultative in many of my communications moving forward.

The idea of asking questions even when I know the answer has become a way of holding others accountable, but also a way for me to stop trying to be so smart. You see, questions, when framed right, will take a conversation in the right direction. This practice irritated my ex-fiance because she felt like I was always trying to challenge her. What I was actually doing was finding ways of not getting frustrated in certain situations.

Here are some steps on how to frame questions with an exercise to practice. I want to use business examples here because I believe that once we learn to speak more in a diplomatic fashion in business, we can transfer the concept into our personal lives.

STEP 1: MASTER THE CONSULTATIVE QUESTIONING FRAMEWORK

Consultative questions focus on *discovery, clarity, and collaboration*. Use this **3-step framework**:

1. **Explore the Situation** – "What is happening right now?"

   - *Example:* "How are you currently handling this process?"

2. **Identify the Impact** – "What's working, what's not?"

- *Example:* "What challenges are these issues creating for your team?"

3. **Guide Toward Possibility** – "What could success look like?"

  - *Example:* "If you could change one thing about this process, what would it be?"

Exercise:

Pick one business scenario (a sales pitch, a staff meeting, or a client consultation). Write three consultative questions using the framework above.

STEP 2: REFRAME OBJECTIONS INTO OPPORTUNITIES

Instead of pushing back, *pivot.* Reframing isn't about proving someone wrong; it's about showing them a new way to look at the same issue.

Formula for Reframing:

1. Acknowledge the concern → *"I hear you."*
2. Reframe with curiosity → *"How do you see this compared to...?"*
3. Invite collaboration → *"What would it take for us to solve this together?"*

Practice Examples:

- Objection: *"We don't have time for this."*

69

- Reframe: *"What's on your plate right now, and how could this actually help ease some of that burden?"*

- Objection: *"We've tried this before, and it didn't work."*

  - Reframe: *"What did you learn from that experience, and how could we approach it differently this time?"*

Exercise:

Write down three objections you commonly hear in your work. For each one, create a reframed question that invites discussion instead of shutting it down.

STEP 3: ROLEPLAY – TURN STATEMENTS INTO QUESTIONS

Statements often sound final. Questions invite dialogue. Here's how to practice flipping them:

- **Statement:** "This is too complicated."

  - **Question:** "Which part feels the most complex to you, and how can I make it easier?"

- **Statement:** "We're not ready yet."

  - **Question:** "What would readiness look like for you, and what steps can we take to get closer?"

Exercise:

Work with a partner. One person throws out a statement. The other must instantly turn it into an open-ended question. Switch roles after five rounds.

STEP 4: REFLECTION AND APPLICATION

- **Self-Check:** In your last important conversation, did you spend more time giving answers or asking questions?
- **Action Plan:** For your next meeting, commit to asking at least *five open-ended questions* before offering any solutions.

Ever notice how attorneys ask questions and how they frame them?

Asking questions can sometimes be meant to trick you into answering them in a way that sounds so literal, so that whatever you say can and will be used against you. The person who asks questions effectively can take control of the conversation. But... asking questions in the wrong way can backfire too.

THE DOUBLE-EDGED SWORD OF QUESTIONS

While questions are powerful, they can also work against you if asked in the wrong way. The intent behind the question matters just as much as the wording. Poorly framed questions can corner, embarrass, or even manipulate others—and once trust is broken, the conversation is hard to recover.

1. Leading Questions Can Corner People

- *"Don't you think this is the best option?"*
- This pressures the other person to agree rather than fostering genuine dialogue.

Exercise: Rewrite this question to make it open and collaborative.

- Instead of: *"Don't you think this is the best option?"*
- Try: _____

2. Rapid-Fire Questions Can Feel Like Interrogation

- *"Why did this happen? Who's at fault? What were you thinking?"*
- Stacked questions overwhelm and make people defensive.

Exercise: Choose one of these rapid-fire questions and reframe it into a calmer, single open-ended question.

- From: *"Who's at fault?"*
- To: _____

3. Loaded Questions Can Be Weaponized

- *"When are you going to get serious about this?"*
- This is less about clarity and more about attack.

Exercise: Reframe this into a neutral, problem-solving question.

- From: *"When are you going to get serious about this?"*
- To: _____

4. Overly Personal Questions Breach Boundaries

- *"Are you even qualified for this role?"*
- Questions framed as judgment damage trust.

Exercise: Imagine you are on the receiving end of this question. Write a calm response that neutralizes the attack.

- Response: _____

HOW TO PROTECT YOURSELF WHEN QUESTIONS ARE USED AGAINST YOU

1. **Pause Before Responding**

   - Silence can be powerful.
   - *Example:* "That's an interesting way to put it— can you clarify what you mean?"

2. **Reframe the Question**

   - Turn it neutral.
   - From: *"Why did you fail at this project?"*
   - To: *"What challenges came up, and how can we address them together?"*

3. **Redirect with Your Own Question**

   - Regain control through curiosity.
   - *Example:* "Before I answer, what's your biggest concern here?"

PRACTICE DRILL: SPOT THE HARMFUL QUESTION

For each of the following, decide if it's a **Helpful Question (HQ)** or a **Harmful Question (XQ)**. If it's harmful, rewrite it.

1. *"What would success look like for you in this role?"* →
   HQ or XQ?
2. *"Why are you always behind schedule?"* → HQ or XQ?
   Rewrite: _____
3. *"How could we make this process easier for your team?"* → HQ or XQ?
4. *"Do you even know what you're doing?"* → HQ or XQ?
   Rewrite: _____

Questions are powerful tools—but like any tool, they can be misused. The best communicators not only master the art of asking the right questions but also practice how to **reframe, neutralize, and redirect harmful ones**.

Now let's go back to the person that I mentioned in earlier to understand how questions can also be a way to truly understand how much of a liar someone can be. Remember when I mentioned how I pretty much felt what I felt, and I was correct? This person has proven to be a pathological liar when confronted with certain questions. They do not realize that the truth was told to me when I was not even looking for it, and by a credible source that truly was looking out for my best interest and to protect me. I noticed the common theme in the answers to the four questions that I asked. I paid attention to their body language and how carefully they spoke.

When we tie in from the previous chapter about understanding how people respond to a text message by ignoring certain points of a conversation, we understand what we are working with. This was an education in dealing with toxic people and the steps to take in order to avoid putting yourself in a bad position. The made-up lies, the way things were framed, the silences, and then the actual, real proof coming from others was enough to understand.

If I had not started to think about the scope of the situation and start asking questions, I would have been a fool. Asking proper questions can unmask the other party and expose them for what they really are. The only true way to better understand and learn where we stand is by asking questions in a way that exposes truths that go far beyond phony conversations and plastic surgeries. My shoulder started to get cold, and I believe that person subconsciously knew it but did not know how to, nor did they care to address it.

In self-reflection, we have to ask ourselves questions and be completely honest. We need to take accountability for our actions and be mindful when we are wrong. We need to maintain curiosity to seek a way to be better. There is always a step or action that is our fault, even when we feel like a mistake or accident was unavoidable.

Things that we might consider:

What landed me in this situation?

What can I do to regain control of the situation?

What can I learn from this?

If I have made the same mistake multiple times, what should I do differently next time?

Once we learn to ask questions, we can take back some control and become a better leaders. Everyone is a leader, but they just do not always realize it because very few sit back and reflect. You learned how to ask questions in business and hopefully understand that you should communicate in a similar fashion in personal interactions, too. My goal is for you to have a healthy frame of mind, read situations effectively, and start taking some power back by asking questions that will help you have a solid backbone in anything that you do!

CHAPTER 9

THE BUSINESS
COMMUNICATOR'S PLAYBOOK

"You don't lead by hitting people over the head—
that's assault, not leadership."
                        — **Dwight D. Eisenhower**

Your communication is your brand.

Every word you say, every pause you take, and every question you ask creates an impression. In business, people don't just buy your product or respect your leadership — they buy into how you communicate. Your communication is your brand. It's how colleagues measure your credibility, how clients decide whether they trust you, and how your team decides if they want to follow you.

This chapter is your playbook: simple, actionable tools you can use every day to elevate how you speak, listen, and influence.

We talked about asking questions in the previous chapter. Here we will dive into more ways to communicate through questions and natural curiosity. Let's start with how we interview for a role. When I speak to people, I learn that many do not know how to hold a conversation. A lot has to do with fear of not being taken seriously. A lot of it has to do with simply not being prepared or well-researched.

All of what I just mentioned can be resolved if we stop and practice to develop our skills. There are so many free resources available to us to motivate us, inspire us, coach us, teach us, and use for skill development that it is actually sad to see how few people take advantage of them. At the time of writing this book, I am personally going through a health improvement and weight loss journey. I have studied what I need to do with my exercises, eating, willpower, and mindset. I took action, and I am doing things I never thought were possible. I am fasting to naturally cure the troubles that started to develop.

A lot of you might think I am doing it wrong and have an opinion, and that is perfectly fine. However, YouTube is my saviour when it comes to inspiring me not to give up. When I am fasting and something feels difficult, I reflect by watching a video to shift my mindset. I am feeling a decade younger, and things are looking up. But I am able to do this by being curious.

I posted a TikTok video with a 30-second snippet teaching high school students how to go out and hunt for opportunities that had over 2,000 comments and 100,000 views. The amount of ignorance and negative comments that went through was outstanding. People come to me with excuses on why my theories do not work, yet when I look at their profile, all they do is waste time putting out foolish content and never devoting time to better themselves!

The bottom line is this! If you want to be taken seriously and respected, you have to do something about it! You need to focus on self-development, and you need to take a 30-second message and seek to find its greater purpose before you become a hater. In this case, you need to become an effective communicator. If you want to get responses to job applications, then work on being creative and selling yourself in the marketplace. Stop expecting things to just naturally come to you!

The business communicators' playbook starts with the decisions and the actions that you choose to take. It is not just about what to say but also about standing out and being unique. The question you need to ask yourself is "Why me?" and this needs to be at the top of mind every single time. Now we are in a time when AI (Artificial Intelligence) is moving at rapid speeds, and many are afraid to be replaced. If you do not want to be replaced, then do something about it and show the value that you bring!

Let's talk about how we can communicate in business.

In every dealership, every boardroom, every sales floor, and every service drive, one truth remains consistent: **communication determines outcomes.** Deals are won or lost because of it. Teams thrive or collapse because of it. Customers stay loyal—or disappear forever—because of it.

Business isn't powered by processes alone. It's powered by the conversations that drive those processes. And if you want to elevate performance, culture, and results, it starts with elevating how people communicate.

This chapter breaks down the core principles of communication mastery—principles that turn ordinary organizations into modern, guest-centric, high-performance operations.

COMMUNICATION WITH PURPOSE

In business, clarity is oxygen. People don't need more words; they need more direction.

Before speaking, writing, or sending any message, ask yourself:

- **What do I want?**
- **Why does it matter?**
- **What action must be taken next?**

Purposeful communication removes friction. It eliminates the endless back-and-forth. It turns reactive employees into proactive contributors.

When communication lacks purpose, organizations drift. When it has direction, organizations move. Think about what your goal is and how you plan to achieve it. Every single time you communicate, you need to be mindful of what the purpose is in the end.

LEAD WITH EMPATHY, NOT EMOTION

Empathy is one of the strongest business tools available today— but most leaders misunderstand it. Empathy isn't softness. It isn't coddling. It's strategic awareness.

It means understanding what someone is experiencing so you can influence the outcome more effectively.

When you say,
"Help me understand what you're dealing with so we can fix it together."

you create partnership instead of resistance.

Empathy unlocks truth.
Truth unlocks solutions.
Solutions unlock performance.

Remember that emotion can create problems and triggers. You must communicate fluently, but also understand that once it turns emotional, it can create issues that we want to avoid.

LISTEN TO UNDERSTAND, NOT TO REACT

Most people listen simply to prepare their reply.

Great communicators listen to uncover the real issue beneath the surface.

They pay attention to:

- tone
- hesitation
- frustration
- patterns
- intentions
- unspoken concerns

This type of listening transforms conversations. It reduces conflict. It builds relationships. Above all, it allows you to solve the correct problem—not just the loudest one.

When leaders develop the discipline to truly listen, their teams rise to match the standard.

DIRECT, NOT AGGRESSIVE

Direct communication is clarity.
Aggressive communication is chaos.

Directness sets expectations.
Aggression destroys trust.

When you say:
"I need these reports completed by 5 PM,"
That's leadership.

When you say:
"Why do I have to keep asking you for this?"

that's emotional leakage.

Business demands high standards. But standards must be delivered with precision, not pressure.

The strongest leaders speak firmly, respectfully, and concisely. They understand that power doesn't come from volume—it comes from clarity.

COMMUNICATING THROUGH
THE RIGHT CHANNELS

Not all communication belongs in all mediums. In fact, many business conflicts begin simply because someone used the wrong channel.

Email is for clarity, documentation, and detail.

Text is for quick confirmations and light-touch follow-up.

Phone calls are for urgency, emotion, and relationship.

Face-to-face conversations are for coaching, leadership, and conflict resolution.

Miscommunication happens not because people don't talk, but because they talk in the wrong way, at the wrong time, through the wrong method.

Great communicators choose the channel that supports the outcome.

THE GUEST EXPERIENCE MINDSET

If there is one mindset shift that elevates business communication above all others, it is this:

Treat people like guests, not transactions.

Guests deserve respect.
Guests deserve clarity.
Guests deserve to feel valued.

When leaders and employees communicate from a guest-centric mindset, everything changes:

- tone improves
- accountability increases
- customers feel the difference
- internal culture strengthens

The guest mindset humanizes the process. It transforms communication from an obligation into an opportunity.

STRUCTURED CONVERSATION: THE 3-PART FRAMEWORK

Strong communicators don't "wing it." They follow a structure. This simple three-step framework will change the way your organization communicates:

1. **Context** – "Here's what's going on."
2. **Expectation** – "Here's what needs to happen."
3. **Accountability** – "Here's how we will follow through."

This model reduces misunderstandings, speeds up execution, and creates a predictable rhythm in your culture.

When people know *how* to communicate, they perform better.

REMOVE THE EGO

Ego is the biggest enemy of effective communication.
Ego wants to be right.
Leadership wants to get it right.

When ego enters the conversation, the mission leaves it. Teams shut down. Creativity evaporates. Accountability collapses.

High-level communicators stay focused on solutions, not pride. They ask questions instead of making assumptions. They maintain control of their state, not their ego.

The moment you remove ego, you open the door to better outcomes. "Ego kills talent" is a line used by Roger James Hamilton on a quote often worn by guitarist Nita Strauss, that reminds us of humility.

ALIGNMENT AND CONFIRMATION

The most expensive phrase in business is:
"I thought you meant…"

Every important conversation should end with confirmation:
"Just so we're aligned…"
"Repeat back the plan so we're on the same page."

This isn't micromanagement—it's quality control.
It prevents rework, resentment, and missed deadlines.

Alignment is the final checkpoint before execution.

CONSISTENCY: THE FINAL PILLAR

Communication becomes culture through repetition.
A one-time message does nothing.
A consistent message changes everything.

Great leaders communicate:

- consistently
- clearly
- calmly
- confidently

Daily communication shapes identity. It sets expectations. It becomes the standard that the entire organization follows.

When communication becomes consistent, leadership becomes effortless. Consistent communication must become the standard in how we communicate every single day.

CLOSING THOUGHT: COMMUNICATION IS YOUR COMPETITIVE EDGE

The companies that win today aren't the ones with the best marketing, the best technology, or even the best product. They're the ones with the best communication. Think about how many roles for guest experience are out there today. This is because the lost art of dealing with people is getting worse as technology grows, and the need to satisfy people continues to grow.

Communication is how you lead.
Communication is how you sell.
Communication is how you create loyalty.
Communication is how you scale.

Master communication—and you master business.

SINGLE-PAGE COMMUNICATION ACTION PLAN **BONUS

1. Daily Clarity

- Hold a 3-minute daily huddle in every department.
- Leaders send a morning priorities message.
- Use standardized email tags:
  ACTION / FYI / QUESTION / URGENT.

2. Guest-Centric Mindset

- Replace "customer" with **"guest."**
- Ask: *"How should this person feel when the conversation ends?"*

- Review communication (calls/emails/texts) monthly for tone and clarity.

3. Clear Communication Framework

Use the 3-step model in every discussion:

1. **Context** – What's going on.
2. **Expectation** – What needs to happen.
3. **Accountability** – Who's doing what, by when.

Finish with: **"Repeat the next steps back to me."**

4. Leadership Communication Excellence

- Send a weekly "state of the team" message.
- Communicate directly, not emotionally.
- Conduct quarterly communication evaluations for leaders.

5. Channel Rules

Use the right medium:

- **Email:** details/documentation
- **Text:** quick confirmations
- **Phone:** urgency or emotion
- **In-person:** coaching and conflict

6. Active Listening Essentials

- Follow the "Listen First" rule.
- Use clarifying statements:
- **"What I'm hearing is…"**
- Score listening skills in call reviews.

7. Ego-Free Culture

- Use no-blame, solution-first meetings.
- Require every problem to come with a proposed solution.
- Train emotional control and tone discipline.

8. Alignment Rituals

- End all conversations with an alignment check.
- Team leads send a daily recap message.
- Use a shared task tracker with color-coded statuses.

9. Continuous Skill Development

- Weekly 20-minute communication drills.
- Monthly role-play sessions.
- Quarterly communication review for all employees.

10. Conflict Resolution Protocol

Follow the 5-step model:

1. Listen
2. Acknowledge
3. Clarify
4. Present solutions
5. Confirm agreement

CHAPTER 10

READING THE ROOM: PERSONAL COMMUNICATION MASTERY

"Silence is a source of great strength."

— *Lao Tzu*

In every interaction—whether at home, with friends, or in business—words tell only a fraction of the story. People rarely communicate their true intentions directly. Instead, they reveal them through energy, tone, facial expressions, posture, and emotional patterns. The art of "reading the room" is the cornerstone of personal communication mastery. It allows you to respond with clarity instead of emotion, influence with confidence, and build deeper, more authentic relationships.

Most people *listen to words.*

Leaders—and emotionally intelligent communicators—listen to **signals.**

This chapter teaches you how to interpret those signals, how to determine the right moment to speak or stay silent, and how to navigate emotionally charged moments with composure and influence.

WHAT THEY SAY MATTERS LESS
THAN WHAT THEY SIGNAL

Human communication is 70% nonverbal. People may say "I'm fine," but their body language reveals tension... or disappointment... or withdrawal. They may agree out loud but resist internally. They may smile while hiding frustration.

When you learn to read what's behind the words, you connect on a deeper level. You understand people better—not just what they say, but who they are in that moment.

Look for the signals:

- Changes in tone
- Slower or faster speech
- Crossed arms, shifting posture
- Avoided eye contact
- Forced or delayed responses
- Overly quick agreement
- Energy drop or energy shift

Reading the room is not about judgment. It's about awareness. It's about seeing the human being behind the conversation. It is about diving in and not being surprised by what might happen. It is about being prepared in the moment to handle any situation.

INTERPRETING TONE AND BODY LANGUAGE AT HOME OR WITH FRIENDS

Personal relationships are where communication habits are shaped—and where they often break down.

To strengthen your personal interactions:

- **Listen for tone changes.** The message behind the message is often in the shift.
- **Watch the body.** Is someone leaning in? Pulling away? Closed off?
- **Observe energy.** Did the mood change after a comment or topic?
- **Notice timing.** Silence often speaks louder than words.

Body language is the emotional soundtrack to the conversation. When you tune into it, you become more empathetic, more connected, and more effective at resolving issues before they escalate.

Example:

If a friend becomes quiet and their posture tightens after you bring something up, don't bulldoze forward. Pause. Acknowledge. Create space.

"Hey, I noticed you went quiet—what's on your mind?"

This level of awareness strengthens trust and deepens connection.

WHEN TO HOLD SPACE AND WHEN TO SPEAK UP

Communication mastery isn't about saying the right thing—it's about saying the right thing **at the right time.**

There are moments when people need answers, and moments when they need silence.

Moments when they need direction, and moments when they need empathy.

To know which one the moment requires, ask yourself:

- Is the person emotionally charged?
- Are they seeking solutions or support?
- Are they venting or asking?
- Are they overwhelmed, frustrated, or disconnected?

Hold space when:

- Someone is emotional or vulnerable
- They need to express themselves without being challenged
- They're processing something difficult
- Advice would feel like pressure

Holding space means giving someone room to be human without rushing or fixing them.

Speak up when:

- Clarity is needed
- Boundaries are crossed

- A solution is expected
- Avoiding the truth would create bigger problems later

Personal communication mastery is knowing the difference.

HANDLING EMOTIONALLY CHARGED MOMENTS

Emotional moments require leadership—not dominance. Your job is to *stabilize the moment*, not escalate it.

Here's the framework:

1. Stay Centered

Control your breathing, your tone, and your volume. Emotional energy multiplies quickly—especially if two people elevate at the same time.

2. Don't Match Their Emotion

Matching intensity escalates conflict. Lowering your energy brings calm into the room.

3. Validate Without Agreeing

Validation isn't surrender—it's acknowledgment.

"I hear you."
"I get why you feel that way."
"This is clearly important to you."

Validation opens the door to logic.

4. Clarify the Real Issue

Often, the surface-level frustration is just the front door. The real emotion is behind it.

Ask:
"What's the real challenge here?"
"What do you need right now?"

5. Respond With Purpose

Never react—respond.

A reaction is emotional.
A response is intentional.

This is how you lead conversations instead of being consumed by them.

THE HEART OF READING THE ROOM

Reading the room is about connection, presence, and emotional intelligence. It's the difference between communicating *at* people and communicating *with* them.

Whether you're at home, with friends, or in the workplace, mastery comes down to:

- Noticing what others miss
- Understanding what others feel
- Responding in a way that builds trust instead of tension

When you can read the room, you elevate every relationship you touch—personally and professionally. You become the calm in the chaos, the clarity in the confusion, and the leader in the moment.

This is communication mastery.

This is emotional leadership.

This is the foundation of influence.

As you can see, there are a lot of layers to uncover. No one said this is going to be easy. How different would things be if I had this kind of knowledge and experience just twenty years ago?

What they say matters less than what they **signal**.

CHAPTER 11

CONFLICT AND PERSPECTIVE: BUILDING BRIDGES, NOT WALLS

> "When we change the way we look at things,
> the things we look at change."
>
> — *Wayne Dyer*

Conflict is inevitable. Misunderstandings happen. Perspectives clash. Emotions surge. But the outcome of any conflict is determined not by the problem itself—but by the approach, the mindset, and the level of emotional intelligence each person brings to the moment.

Most people react to conflict with instinct, not intention. They protect their ego, defend their position, and build emotional walls. These walls may feel safe in the moment, but they isolate, disconnect, and damage relationships. Building walls is easy.

This is where self-reflection plays a crucial role in communication. While it may seem that we are walking on eggshells to show a side of us, it really only means that we are mature and open-minded.

Building bridges takes leadership.

The real power lies in managing conflict through the lens of perspective—seeing not only your truth, but someone else's.

That's where communication evolves. That's where relationships grow. That's where trust deepens.

THE DIFFERENCE BETWEEN A WALL AND A BRIDGE

A **wall** is built from fear, ego, defensiveness, or pride.

A **bridge** is built from understanding, patience, and intention.

Walls divide.

Bridges connect.

Conflict becomes destructive when people dig into their corner, guard their beliefs, and refuse to hear anything beyond their own viewpoint. It becomes constructive when people step forward with curiosity instead of accusation, and with perspective instead of emotion.

A simple truth:

You don't have to agree with someone to understand them.

Understanding is the foundation of every bridge. When we understand, we are more prone to discovering other solutions and creating a better bridge.

PERSPECTIVE: THE MISSING LAYER IN MOST CONFLICTS

Most conflict occurs not because of what happened, but because of what it **meant** to each person.

Two people experience the same moment differently:

- One sees disrespect.
- The other sees urgency.
- One sees criticism.
- The other sees guidance.
- One feels attacked.
- The other feels ignored.

Perspective shapes interpretation. Interpretation shapes emotion. Emotion shapes behavior.

The moment you acknowledge that every person's perspective is filtered through their past experiences, beliefs, fears, and expectations, you unlock the ability to communicate with compassion instead of conflict.

Perspective turns you from a fighter into a facilitator.

UNDERSTANDING BEFORE ARGUING

Conflict becomes productive the moment someone chooses to understand before arguing. This is the leadership mindset that transforms tension into teamwork.

To build that bridge:

- Ask questions instead of making assumptions.
- Get curious about the other person's viewpoint.
- Listen for meaning, not just words.
- Seek to understand their experience of the moment.

Replace

"What's your problem?"
with
"Help me understand how you saw it."

Replace

"You're wrong."
with
"Can you walk me through your perspective?"

Understanding does not equal agreement. It simply opens the door to resolution.

WHY EGO MAKES WALLS HIGHER

Ego is the architect of every emotional wall.

When ego leads:

- We escalate instead of de-escalate.
- We defend instead of understand.
- We react instead of respond.
- We focus on being right instead of getting it right.

Ego destroys collaboration.

When you remove ego, you create space—space for solutions, clarity, and connection.

The strongest person in any conflict is the one who can stay calm, stay curious, and stay in control of themselves.

HOW TO BUILD BRIDGES IN MOMENTS OF TENSION

Here is the bridge-building framework:

1. Pause Before Responding

When emotion rises, logic falls. Take a moment. Breathe. Reset. A calm mind builds better bridges.

2. Acknowledge Their Perspective

Not their accuracy—their *experience.*

"I hear you."
"I understand why you felt that way."
"Thank you for sharing that."

Validation is not agreement—it is respect.

3. Share Your Perspective Clearly

Without blame. Without aggression. Without accusation.

Use "I" statements.
Stay focused on the issue, not the person.

4. Identify the True Source of the Conflict

Most arguments are symptoms, not causes.
Ask: "What's the real issue here?"

5. Reset the Conversation

Shift from "me vs. you" to "us vs. the problem."
"What's a solution that works for both of us?"

"How do we move forward together?"

6. Set Clear Agreements

Bridges collapse without structure.
Finish with clarity on next steps and commitments.

TURNING CONFLICT INTO CONNECTION

The most powerful relationships—personal or professional—aren't defined by the absence of conflict. They're defined by how conflict is navigated.

When handled with emotional intelligence:

- Conflict deepens understanding
- Conflict strengthens trust
- Conflict elevates communication
- Conflict builds maturity

People respect you not because you avoid conflict, but because you handle it with purpose, stability, and perspective.

THE LEADERSHIP MINDSET: FROM RESISTANCE TO RESOLUTION

Leaders solve tension, not by overpowering people, but by connecting with them. They look past the immediate emotion and focus on the long-term relationship. They choose clarity over chaos. They choose growth over ego. They choose bridges over walls.

And when you develop this mindset—at home, at work, and in your inner circle—you become someone others look to in difficult moments. You become a stabilizer, not an inflamer. You become the one who turns resistance into resolution.

This is where influence lives.
This is where maturity grows.
This is where real communication happens.

When people don't understand, they defend. I am not saying that you need to be high and mighty, but you should be smart and agile with how you approach situations.

CHAPTER 12

WORDS THAT WIN: PERSONAL AND PROFESSIONAL WORD TRACKS

"Words may show a man's wit, but actions his meaning."

— Benjamin Franklin

Words are more than sounds—they are tools of influence. They can open doors or close them. Strengthen relationships or weaken them. Calm emotions or ignite conflict. In every interaction, the language you choose becomes a reflection of your mindset, your emotional intelligence, and your leadership.

People often think success comes from speaking more.

In reality, success comes from speaking **better**.

The right words build connection, trust, clarity, and momentum. The wrong words trigger defensiveness, confusion, and resistance. Mastering communication isn't about memorizing scripts—it's about using **intentional word tracks** that guide conversations toward clarity and collaboration.

This chapter equips you with the personal and professional phrases that make you more effective in every area of life—

from relationships to leadership to business. After looking at different methods, this is where you will start to shine.

WHY WORD TRACKS MATTER

A great word track does three things:

1. **Reduces emotional tension**
2. **Creates clarity and direction**
3. **Builds trust and partnership**

People respond not just to *what* you say, but to *how* you say it. A strong communicator understands how language shapes energy, tone, and outcome.

When you master word tracks, you master influence—and influence is the currency of leadership.

PERSONAL WORD TRACKS: STRENGTHENING CONNECTION AND UNDERSTANDING

Relationships thrive on communication, and communication thrives on emotional clarity. These word tracks help you create a deeper connection and reduce misunderstanding.

1. "Help me understand…"

This softens any conversation and opens the door to truth without accusation.

2. "What I'm hearing is…"

Great for confirmation, empathy, and preventing misinterpretation.

3. "Is this a moment to listen or a moment to help solve?"

A powerful tool for partners, friends, or family members.

4. "I'm here. Take your time."

A grounding phrase for someone overwhelmed or emotional.

5. "Let's talk about what you *need* right now."

Moves the conversation from emotion to clarity.

These aren't scripts—they're emotional stabilizers. They help you stay connected when tension enters the room.

PROFESSIONAL WORD TRACKS: LEADING, SELLING, AND COMMUNICATING WITH CONFIDENCE

In business, people follow confidence, clarity, and composure. These word tracks elevate your professionalism instantly.

1. "Here's what I can do for you."

Shifts focus from problems to solutions.

2. "Let's align on expectations before we move forward."

Prevents miscommunication and sets standards.

3. "What outcome are you hoping for?"

Clarifies the target before offering direction.

4. "Let's look at this together."

Creates a partnership instead of a hierarchy.

5. "Here's the next step…"

Provides leadership, structure, and momentum.

These phrases make communication clean, direct, and outcome-driven.

WORD TRACKS FOR CONFLICT: TURNING TENSION INTO TRUST

When emotions rise, logic drops. These word tracks keep conversations productive instead of reactive.

1. "I hear you—and I want to understand your perspective."

Validates without surrendering.

2. "Let's slow down for a moment."

Resets the emotional temperature.

3. "What's the real challenge here?"

Uncovers the root issue, not just the surface complaint.

4. "We're on the same team. Let's solve this together."

Reframes the dynamic from adversarial to collaborative.

5. "What's a solution that works for both of us?"

Shifts ownership and encourages collaboration.

These are bridge-building phrases—simple but powerful.

WORD TRACKS FOR LEADERSHIP: GUIDING WITH PURPOSE AND PRESENCE

Leadership language must carry weight, calm, and clarity. These word tracks elevate your presence.

1. "Here's what success looks like..."

Defines the target with certainty.

2. "Tell me how you would approach this."

Encourages ownership and creativity.

3. "I appreciate your effort—let's refine the direction."

Corrects without discouraging.

4. "How can I support you better?"

Builds trust and loyalty.

5. "Let's walk through this together."

Shows partnership without micromanagement.

Leadership is not loud—it's intentional.

WORD TRACKS FOR ACCOUNTABILITY: HOLDING STANDARDS—RESPECTFULLY

Accountability is where most people struggle. These word tracks make it easier and more constructive.

1. "Let's review the expectations we agreed on."

Removes emotion and focuses on agreements.

2. "Help me understand what prevented this from happening."

Uncovers issues without blame.

3. "What's your plan to correct this?"

Promotes ownership.

4. "Let's set a timeline for the next step."

Adds structure and clarity.

5. "Do you feel clear on the expectations moving forward?"

Ensures alignment.

Accountability becomes smoother when the language is firm but respectful.

WHY THESE WORD TRACKS WORK

These phrases work because they:

- Reduce emotional defensiveness
- Build clarity and alignment
- Encourage collaboration
- Maintain respect and dignity
- Shift the conversation toward progress

They help you stay in control of the *moment* so you can guide the *outcome*.

Words have power. And when you use the right words, you elevate your relationships, your leadership, and your influence.

FINAL INSIGHT: YOUR LANGUAGE SHAPES YOUR LEGACY

How you speak becomes how people remember you.

Your words shape your reputation.
Your tone shapes your influence.
Your communication shapes your impact.

When you learn to speak with the intention of connection, collaboration, and clarity, your world changes. People trust you more. They follow you more. They open up to you more. Problems dissolve faster. Relationships deepen. Results improve.

The right words don't just win conversations—they win people.

And when you win people, you win in life and in business.

WORD TRACKS CHEAT SHEET

Words That Win in Personal & Professional Communication

1. Connection & Understanding

Use these to build rapport, empathy, and emotional clarity:

- "Help me understand…"
- "What I'm hearing is…"
- "Tell me more about what you mean."
- "Is this a moment to listen or a moment to help solve?"
- "I'm here. Take your time."

2. Leadership & Clarity

These tracks create structure, direction, and alignment:

- "Here's what success looks like…"
- "Let's align on expectations."
- "Here's the next step…"
- "Tell me how you would approach this."
- "How can I support you better?"

3. Conflict & Emotional Moments

Use these phrases to de-escalate and rebuild connection:

- "I hear you—and I want to understand your perspective."
- "Let's slow down for a moment."
- "What's the real challenge here?"
- "We're on the same team—let's solve this together."

- "What's a solution that works for both of us?"

4. Accountability & Performance

Hold standards respectfully and clearly:

- "Let's review the expectations we agreed on."
- "Help me understand what prevented this from happening."
- "What's your plan to correct this?"
- "Let's set a timeline for the next step."
- "Do you feel clear on expectations moving forward?"

5. Professional Excellence (BDC, Sales, Leadership)

These elevate your tone, confidence, and influence:

- "Here's what I can do for you…"
- "Let's look at this together."
- "What outcome are you hoping for?"
- "I appreciate your effort—let's refine the direction."
- "Let me clarify the process for you."

6. Personal Relationships

Strengthen emotional connection at home or with friends:

- "I want to understand your feelings first."
- "What do you need from me right now?"
- "Let's work through this together."
- "I didn't realize that affected you—thank you for telling me."
- "Your feelings matter to me."

REMINDER:

The right words don't just win conversations—

They win trust, relationships, and results.

CHAPTER 13

YOUR PERSONAL COMMUNICATION ACTION PLAN

"To know oneself is to study oneself in action with another person."

— *Bruce Lee*

I t's time to walk the talk.

Mastering communication is not about talent—it's about intentional habits practiced consistently. The way you speak, listen, respond, and interpret signals shapes the quality of every relationship in your life. Communication is the foundation of influence, trust, leadership, and emotional stability. And like any skill, it grows through discipline.

This chapter gives you a personal communication action plan—a simple, powerful roadmap for becoming a more effective communicator at home, with friends, and in your professional life. These steps help you level up your presence, clarity, and emotional intelligence so you can navigate conversations with confidence and purpose.

It is simple! If it does not help me in any way, I stay quiet these days. Suppose I can influence change in the most positive way,

I do it slowly and carefully. The lessons learned here should not take a lifetime to learn. What has taken me over twenty years to learn, I am leaving here with you now.

WHY YOU NEED A PERSONAL COMMUNICATION PLAN

Communication touches everything:

- How you resolve conflict
- How you connect with loved ones
- How you lead your team
- How you handle pressure
- How you express your needs
- How you influence outcomes

Without a plan, communication becomes reactive—driven by emotion instead of intention. With a plan, communication becomes a strength—a tool you can rely on in every situation.

This chapter moves communication from something you do to something you **master**.

STEP 1: DEFINE YOUR COMMUNICATION IDENTITY

Before you can improve, you must understand who you are when you communicate today.

Ask yourself:

- How do others usually experience me?
- Do I speak clearly or emotionally?

- Do I listen fully or prepare my reply?
- Do I lead conversations or react to them?
- Do people feel heard after speaking with me?

Your identity drives your habits.
Your habits drive your results.

Choose the communicator you want to become.

STEP 2: MASTER THE PAUSE

The pause is the most powerful tool in communication.

It prevents overreaction.
It gives you time to think.
It keeps emotions from hijacking the moment.

Before responding—pause.
Before assuming—pause.
Before escalating—pause.

One second can save a relationship.

One breath can save a conversation.

The pause is where maturity enters.

STEP 3: PRACTICE ACTIVE LISTENING

Listening is the foundation of influence.

To level up your listening:

- Make eye contact
- Put your phone down

- Give verbal acknowledgment ("I hear you...")
- Ask clarifying questions
- Reflect back on what you heard

Listening is not silence—it's presence.

When you listen at a higher level, people trust you at a deeper level.

STEP 4: USE INTENTIONAL WORD TRACKS

Your words carry weight.
Your tone carries emotion.
Your phrasing carries influence.

Adopt intentional word tracks such as:

- "Help me understand..."
- "What I'm hearing is..."
- "Let's align on expectations..."
- "What outcome are you hoping for?"
- "Here's the next step..."

These word tracks guide conversations toward clarity, not confusion.

They help you stay calm, stay centered, and stay in control.

STEP 5: COMMUNICATE WITH STRUCTURE

Clear communication follows a predictable pattern.

Use the **3-Part Clarity Framework:**

1. **Context** – What's going on
2. **Expectation** – What needs to happen
3. **Accountability** – Who's responsible and by when

This structure eliminates confusion and makes every conversation easier.

Whether you're talking to a partner, a child, a friend, or a team member—structure builds certainty.

STEP 6: LEARN TO READ THE ROOM

People communicate through more than words.

Their body language, tone, and energy tell the real story.

To read the room:

- Watch posture
- Listen for tone shifts
- Notice changes in energy or mood
- Pay attention to silence
- Look for discomfort or hesitation

Reading the room allows you to respond appropriately, not impulsively.

It transforms you from a talker into a communicator.

STEP 7: CHOOSE BRIDGES OVER WALLS

In moments of tension, you have a choice:

Build a bridge or build a wall.

Walls are built with:

- Ego
- Assumption
- Accusation
- Defensiveness

Bridges are built with:

- Curiosity
- Validation
- Calmness
- Perspective

Ask:

- "Can you walk me through how you saw it?"
- "I want to understand your experience."
- "What's a solution that works for both of us?"

Conflict becomes easier when the goal is connection, not victory.

STEP 8: STAY CONSISTENT

Communication mastery is a practice—not a one-time decision.

Commit to:

- Daily moments of intentional communication
- Weekly reflection on your tone and presence
- Monthly recalibration of your habits
- Ongoing refinement of your word tracks

Consistency turns practice into identity.

STEP 9: REFLECT AFTER KEY CONVERSATIONS

Reflection sharpens awareness.

After emotional or important conversations, ask:

- What did I do well?
- What could I have done differently?
- Did I listen enough?
- Did I respond with intention or emotion?
- Did the other person feel understood?

Growth lives in reflection.

STEP 10: BUILD A PERSONAL COMMUNICATION CODE

Your code is a set of personal commitments that define how you show up in conversation.

Examples:

- "I will respond calmly, not react emotionally."
- "I will listen fully before I speak."
- "I will seek understanding before giving direction."
- "I will choose clarity over comfort."
- "I will use my words to build connection, not conflict."

This code becomes your compass.

YOUR NEW STANDARD OF COMMUNICATION

Communication mastery is not perfection—it's intention.

It's showing up differently.
It's speaking with purpose.
It's listening with presence.
It's understanding before responding.
It's leading with emotional intelligence, not ego.

Your personal communication action plan is your roadmap to:

- deeper relationships
- calmer conversations
- stronger leadership
- better decisions
- greater influence
- more trust
- and a more grounded version of yourself

When you improve your communication, you improve your entire life.

COMMUNICATE RIGHT, LIVE RIGHT

As we come to an end, you are probably wondering, How do I put this all together? How do I piece this all together? But more importantly, how long does it take to make a change?

Before we start thinking about change management, we need to reflect on our interactions with others. Think about why you might be hurting other people emotionally. You see, we are born into this world without knowing or truly understanding how or why we are being treated a certain way. In the world we live in today, many families operate beyond normal expectations.

As I finish writing this book, I am single because I know what is on the other side until I meet someone who can prove me wrong. We do not communicate effectively with one another anymore. Also, when we do speak up, everyone gets offended. More of us should start meditating and reflecting on where we are in life. Life is very short, and it cannot be wasted on doing the same thing over and over again.

To be competent and effective communicators, we should all be mindful of the situations we face. Do you ever just sit back with a cup of coffee and people-watch? I am talking about just watching the room, noticing how people speak to one another, thinking about what they are saying, and wondering why they say things the way they do. I ask this question because it is interesting to hear others' experiences of people watching.

I like watching scenarios in car dealerships because I am like a human profit-leak finder. For example, I want to stand behind a wall and listen to how a deal is being worked. I pay attention to the questions being asked and to how the back-and-forth is going. To give you an example, I constantly find money being lost because communication is unclear. I'm curious why the sales manager just put $1,500 extra into a car without taking the time to work the deal. If you are a dealership manager and you are not analyzing situations with questions, you are in the wrong business.

In any line of work, not asking questions will lead to a loss of profit. But it is how we ask the question, even when we already know the answer, that adds professionalism to the situation at hand. Think about how you work with other departments and teams. What kinds of questions can you ask them to show that you are simply listening to them?

On a personal level, you may need to reconnect with someone you've lost touch with to reignite the energy that once existed. Remember how short life is, and remember to look at situations from various sides before you just pass judgment, just like the person I mentioned a few times throughout this book. I understand you a lot more as a person because of what you went through. You do not trust easily because you are careful not to be hurt, lied to, or anything else that you have endured. I am here to tell you that we are not all bad. Every conversation is a fork in the road: disconnect or deepen.

This book is a roadmap, but your actions are the journey. Mastering communication is mastering **how you lead, how you love, and how you grow**. Communicate right, and you won't just win arguments. You'll win trust, relationships, and the kind of life most people only hope for.

It was an honor to present you with this modern interpretation of something that has existed for ages. There are plenty of books that you could have read, and I hope that you do read them. However, this is my take on communication skills and reading the situation. Now, in 2025, we need this kind of education because human interaction is becoming increasingly complex.

I want you to bring back more human interaction with less judgment of what we find. I want us all to think with an open mind and learn to understand what is going on around us. At the same time, I want you to be thoughtful and intentional.

My stories at the beginning of the book helped inspire you and coach you into understanding situations. As we delve deeper into it, you will notice how much the book changes. I did this because I wanted to truly immerse you in various ways of handling situations. I hope that you never stop learning and continue to seek more effective ways to be a competent communicator.